THE INDIAN'S WEEK

A Book to Color

THE INDIAN'S WEEK

Written by Lorraine Long and Mary Lou Roberts
Illustrated by Lisa K. Walraven

The Sing to Read Adventure
The Indian's Week
Text copyright © 1995 by Lorraine Long
Published by Periwinkle Park Educational Productions
3217 Eagle Watch Drive, Woodstock, Georgia 30189

Printed in the United States in 1998 by
Image Graphics Incorporated
Paducah, Kentucky 42002

Layout Assistance, Bill Regenberg

Edited by Kirsten Taylor

Sunday, Sunday,

guess what he wore?

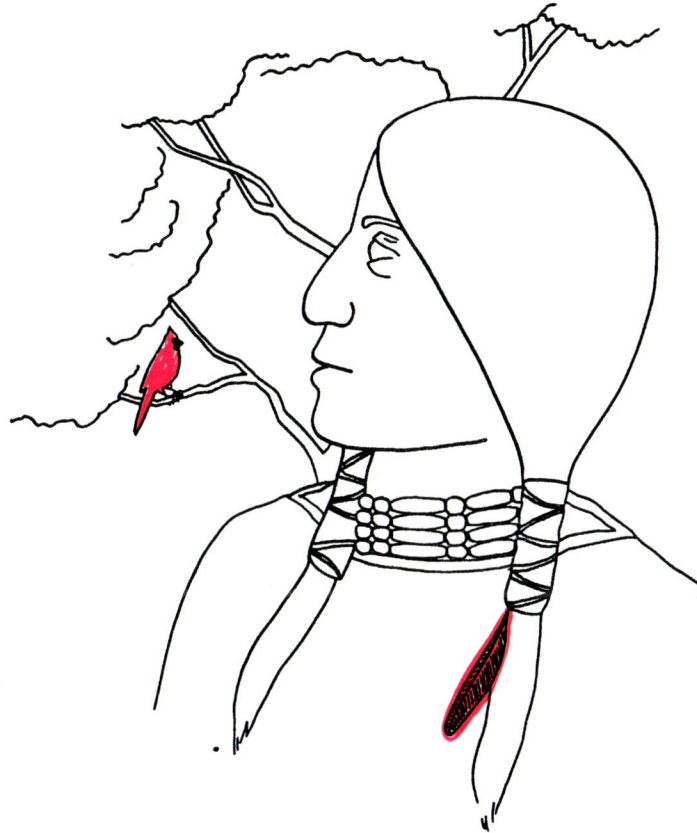

One red feather and no more.

Monday, Monday, guess what he wore?

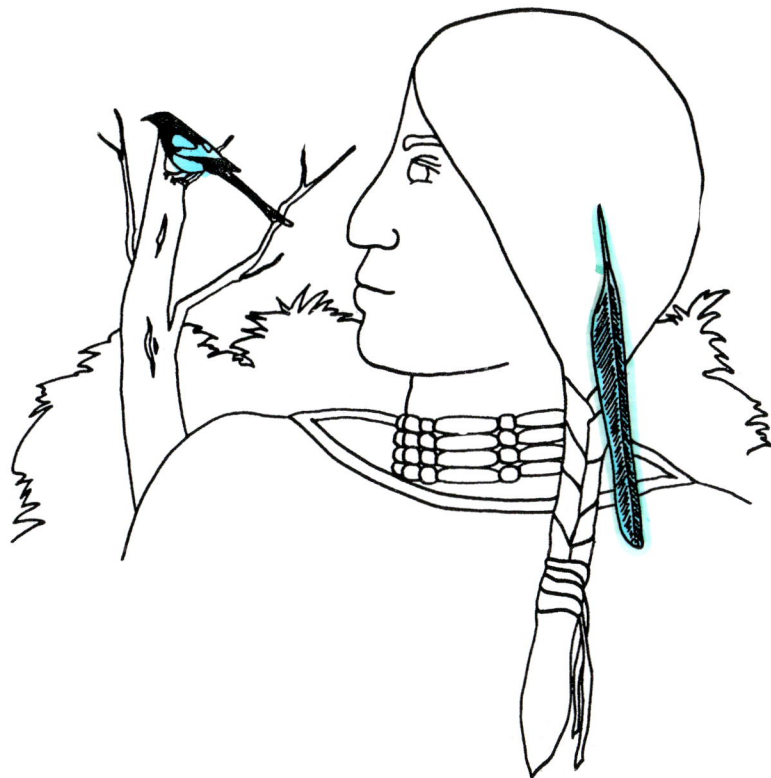

One blue feather and no more.

Tuesday, Tuesday,

guess what he wore?

One green feather and no more.

Wednesday, Wednesday, guess what he wore?

One yellow feather and no more.

Thursday, Thursday,

guess what he wore?

One purple feather and no more.

Friday, Friday,

guess what he wore?

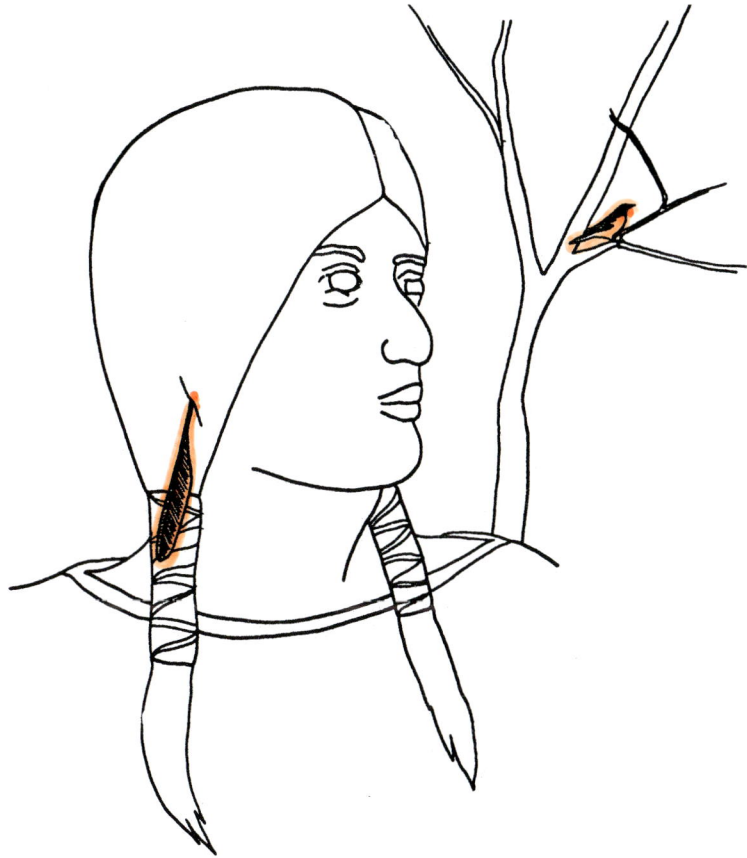

One orange feather and no more.

Saturday, Saturday,

he wore them all.

The Indian brave stood proud and tall.

The End, Friend

Teaching Facts

- Native Americans were the first inhabitants of the Americas. They came 20,000 years ago, thousands of years before any Europeans arrived.

- Native American family life centered around providing life's necessities: food, clothing and shelter.

- Native Americans hunted and fished for food. Those who farmed raised corn, beans and squash. Other crops included potatoes, peanuts, peppers and tomatoes.

- Native Americans usually made clothing from animal skins.

- Native Americans engaged in many arts and crafts, including pottery, basketry, carving, weaving and painting.

- Native American girls and boys had chores to do.
  Native American Girls:
  - They watched their mothers and grandmothers to learn how to cook, sew and take care of the children.
  - They were taught how to plant and tend fields, gather nuts and berries and prepare food.
  - They learned to tan deer skin and turn it into clothing.
  - They learned to use clay to make pots and beads for necklaces.

  Native American Boys:
  - They were taught to hunt deer and bear, fish the streams and rivers and trap small animals.
  - They learned to make arrows from branches, and would add sharp points with bones and rocks.
  - It was their job to collect firewood from the forests, fetch water from nearby streams and chase birds away from the fields.

Birds featured in the book

Cover Illustration - Black Billed Magpie

Sunday, red feather - Cardinal

Monday, blue feather - Black Billed Magpie

Tuesday, green feather - Green Winged Teal

Wednesday, yellow feather - Summer Tanager (female)

Thursday, purple feather - Grackle

Friday, orange feather - Northern Oriole

Saturday - Bald Eagle

Math - Native American Necklace

Materials: 30 " pieces of yarn
(one per child)
rubbing alcohol
food coloring (3 different colors)
newspaper
3 large plastic bags that seal
cookie sheets
masking tape
ziti, penne rigate or mostaccioli rigati pasta
(Brands may vary in size;
choose the largest for easy threading.)

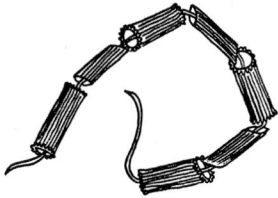

Skills: sorting
patterning
fine motor

Adult preparation:

1. Dye the pasta using the 3 different colors of food coloring. Put one third of the pasta into one of the plastic bags. Pour about 1/2 cup of alcohol into the bag with several drops of one color of food coloring. Mix the pasta, alcohol and food coloring in the plastic bag. Let the pasta sit in the plastic bag, turning every 10 minutes until the pasta is a vibrant color.
2. Repeat the dying process for the other two colors.
3. When the pasta is vibrant in color, pour the alcohol out of the bag. Line a cookie sheet with newspaper. Lay the pasta on the newspaper to dry for 2 hours.

4. Prepare the yarn necklace by tearing off a small piece of masking tape and twisting it around one end of the yarn to make a pointed threading needle.

Directions for the child:
1. Adult - Explain to your child that Native American children made their own jewelry. You are going to create your own Native American necklace.
2. Sort the pasta by color by making small piles of each color on the table.
3. Look at all of the colors.
4. Can you create your own patterns with these colors?
> Example: ABAB - red, blue, red, blue
> ABCABC - red, green, yellow, red, green, yellow
> AABBAABB - red, red, blue, blue, red, red, blue, blue

Lay the colored patterns on the table in a row.
5. Choose a pattern you like best to string onto your necklace.

Adult assistance:
1. After your child has completed stringing, tie the two ends together to make the necklace.

Adult questions:
1. Ask your child to show you the pattern she or he used for the necklace.
2. Ask your child to say the color pattern and then ask how that pattern can be represented by alphabet letters (e.g. ABAB, ABCABC, AABBAABB).

Art - Native American Blanket

Materials:

muslin cloth
  (cut into 18 " x 18" squares,
  one per child)
permanent black marker
tempera paint of different colors
medium to large artist brushes
1 large cardboard box
push pins
yarn (any color, 7" strands)
yard stick
water
flat surface
scissors
small plastic bowls for each color of paint
  (Margarine tubs with lids are the perfect size.)

Skills:

fine motor
creative design

Adult preparation:

1. Take apart the cardboard box so that you can lay the muslin out on it and secure it with push pins.
2. Mix the paint with a little bit of water in the plastic bowl. Use a plastic bowl for each color being mixed.

Directions for the child:

1. Adult - Explain to your child that Native Americans created their own blanket designs and patterns. Each tribe had unique designs.
2. You are going to design your own Native American blanket.
3. You are going to use a yardstick to make the line design on your Native American blanket.
4. Lay the yardstick anywhere on the muslin cloth and use the black marker to draw a line against the yardstick across the cloth. Pick up the yardstick and lay it on the cloth in a different direction. Draw a line again with the black marker. Do this as many times as you wish until you get a design you like.
5. Observe the new shapes you created. You are going to paint inside each shape with the different paint colors.
6. Choose your colors carefully so that each shape is surrounded by different colors.
7. When your whole blanket is painted, let it dry pinned down on the cardboard.

Adult assistance:

1. When the blanket is dry, remove the push pins.
2. Use the scissors to snip a small hole in each corner.
3. Thread four strands of yarn through one of the corner holes and tie to make a tassel.
4. Repeat the tassel directions for each corner of the blanket.
5. Display your child's Native American blanket.

Curriculum incorporated:

- Rhyme
- Days of the week
- Native Americans
- Punctuation - question mark
- Tracking left to right
- Whole book success
- Parts of a book - cover
    - back
    - title page
    - dedication page
- What an author does
- What an illustrator does

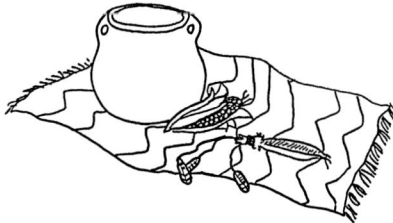

The cover illustration for this
book was done in oil pastels.

THE INDIAN'S WEEK

Sunday, Sunday, guess what he wore?
One red feather and no more.

Monday, Monday, guess what he wore?
One blue feather and no more.

Tuesday, Tuesday, guess what he wore?
One green feather and no more.

Wednesday, Wednesday, guess what he wore?
One yellow feather and no more.

Thursday, Thursday, guess what he wore?
One purple feather and no more.

Friday, Friday, guess what he wore?
One orange feather and no more.

Saturday, Saturday, he wore them all.
The Indian brave stood proud and tall.